The Book of
Star Light

The Book of
Star Light

White Eagle

THE WHITE EAGLE PUBLISHING TRUST
NEW LANDS · LISS · HAMPSHIRE · ENGLAND

First published December 1999
© Copyright, the White Eagle Publishing Trust, 1999

British Library Cataloguing-in-Publication Data
A catalogue record for this book is available from
the British Library

ISBN 0-85487-118-7

Artist, Gaynor Goffe
with house designers

For a full list of White Eagle publications contact The
White Eagle Publishing Trust at New Lands, Brewells
Lane, Liss, Hampshire, GU33 7HY. In the Americas
write to P O Box 930, Montgomery, Texas 77356,
USA; and in Australasia to P O Box 225, Maleny,
Queensland 4552, Australia. Alternatively, visit our
website: http://www.whiteeaglepublishing.org.

Set in Arepo by the publisher and printed and bound
in Great Britain at the University Press, Cambridge

Introduction

This is a very different book from most of the volumes you will find in a bookshop. It is not yet another book about self-help and still less a textbook. Yet it offers a way in which each one of us can bring real service to the world, and by which we can transform ourselves and our lives. Of course it is a spiritual book, because it may touch the deepest spirit in each of its readers; and we hope in fact that the words will come across to each reader with freshness and freedom. It centres around one particular symbol, a six-pointed Star, and yet it is a book of real warmth and heart. It can be read right through from cover to cover, but it is really meant to give strength again and again no matter what page it is which you open.

It is offering every one of us the simplest thing on earth: a way to find the place inside ourselves which orders our thoughts, creates health in the body, and allows us to find healing and radiate it throughout our own being, to people we know, and to the world. This is an almost incredibly simple idea, and yet thousands of people have been benefitting from putting it into practice for many years already.

What is the Star mentioned in the title? A symbol: a very ancient symbol, but one whose meaning is being understood on more and more levels. Maybe it is a symbol for the millennium ahead. A Star can have any number of points, but it is the six-pointed Star which is the perfect geometrical figure, and it is the six-pointed Star which symbolizes perfection. It is composed of an upward-pointing and a downward-pointing equilateral triangle. The two triangles are fused into one perfect Star with no dividing lines, no complexity, radiating light. You can see it as a simple two-dimensional figure, or even more beautifully, as a three-dimensional one: two triangular pyramids fused and interlocking.*

A figure that symbolizes perfection? Does perfection sound rather a remote possibility? The idea of the Star is that however imperfect we may feel from day to day, we all contain within us a tiny Star, the seed of our own perfection. Bring the consciousness to it, and it immediately starts to grow.

Perfection of health, perfection of our being, perfection of the world in which we live: they are all things which we strive for. But the thought of perfection is already there in our consciousness, a little Star within. That is exactly what the Star is: the thought of perfection in our consciousness. At this point it is no longer a symbol, it is an element of our consciousness. It is alive, creative, vibrant.

So to see the Star in our imagination is actually to be in touch with the perfect being that we are, however imperfect we may feel with our minds! You can see the Star above you, filling you with light; you can see that Star within you, radiating light; or you can see

*See the website mentioned at the end of this introduction.

yourself as the Star, so that with your whole being you *are* the Star, radiating light. If you have someone close to you who seems in need of healing, your very radiation of the Star, in your imagination, will reach them. If you have fears and worries about conditions in the world, your radiation of the light will help to bring peace. It will guide the situation forward to an eventually beautiful outworking, however long that takes. You are never powerless when you work with the Star. From the same source as the quotations in this book, 'Every one of you is your own saviour, and every one of you is the saviour of all human kind'.

And what *is* the source of the words in the book? White Eagle is simply the name under which these words were given. It does not matter who he is, and the gift of the symbol of the Star comes in any case from the very deepest source. White Eagle is the messenger for the wise ones who have given this for our use.

The sayings in the book suggest using the Star whenever you like. Concentration on the Star can be built up into a regular practice. You can think of it every day on waking, or several times a day, until this thought has become a self-renewing habit. Visualizing the Star is something that combines well with meditation practice, or with conventional prayer, but it is perfectly powerful on its own. It is an ideal focus for concentration when you are working with others to visualize or pray for peace, whether that is in a religious context or whether you are 'tuning in' to some appointed day of special attention to peace or earth-healing. You may wish to be specially quiet when you focus on the Star. You may choose to light a candle and relax gently as you gaze at the flame. You might alternatively use an open rose as a starting point until your focus changes and it becomes to you a Star; one of the sayings suggests this. But however you go about it, there is no moment when you cannot contact the Star, so long as you wish to.

Further help with using the Star can be found through a world-wide Star Link network. See the web site http://www.thestarlink.net. There is a beautiful three-dimensional Star image at this site to help. The Star Link is administered by the White Eagle Lodge, an organisation based around the White Eagle teaching. You can also be read about it in literature to be had from The Star Link, New Lands, Brewells Lane, Liss, Hampshire, England GU33 7HY (e-mail stars@thestarlink.net). In the USA, you can also write to the Star Link at PO Box 930, Montgomery, Texas 77356; and in Australasia, to PO Box 225, Maleny, Queensland 4552.

The same addresses will offer more information about the teaching which has given birth to the Star Link, that of the White Eagle Lodge, and the other books published in White Eagle's name.

Above you is a Star
of infinite light,
beauty, power and love.
From this Star the light is
pouring down upon you.
Attune yourself to this
central point of power.
It is your life.

*As you open heart
and mind and your
whole being to the Star,
the outer self becomes
radiant in the light of the
Star. All worry, all dis-
quiet drops away as you
bathe in this beautiful
golden light.*

*The Star, which is
a symbol of the highest
life, is within your heart
as well as blazing in
the heavens. You are all
small stars: you are
building the Star of life
within your own soul.*

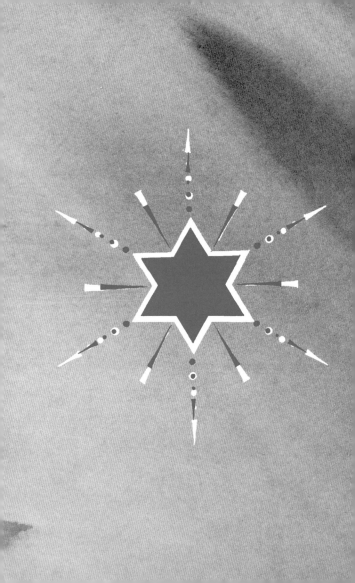

The Star shines down upon you. Feel the rays of the Star, penetrating your heart. Just gently breathe in the rays, absorb into every cell of your being the rays of that glorious Star. Be still under the Star.

As you learn to become
peaceful under the Star,
you radiate this peace
into the outer world.

The Star is not only a great
cosmic power, it is also a
tender, loving, guiding
power; a protecting power in
your life. If you can
surrender yourself to the
sweet and lovely Star
radiance, you will find that
your pathway will be one of
light and happiness and
gentle peace. All your needs
are understood and you will
receive the comfort, the
guidance and the love that
you need as you go
into the Star.

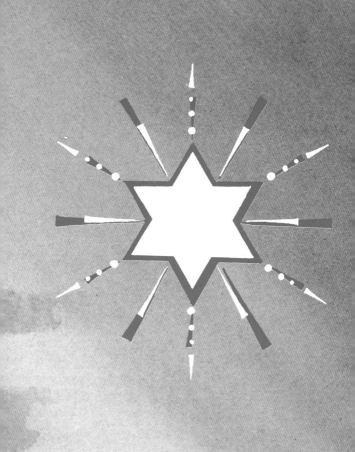

*Quietly breathe—
very gently—and as you
breathe, feel that you are
absorbing into every cell of
your being the rays of the
glorious Star shining just
above you.... Just breathe
peacefully, and feel this
wonderful light of the Star
filling your heart with every
breath you take.*

Create the form of the six-pointed Star in your heart.... If you visualize and create that form in your heart, or in the mind within the heart, you then do it in deep love. This love is sometimes understood more easily if you will become aware of a beautiful rose with an exquisite perfume that immediately brings to mind thoughts of tranquillity and beauty.... The Star that you create is built up by this subtle essence of love within your heart.

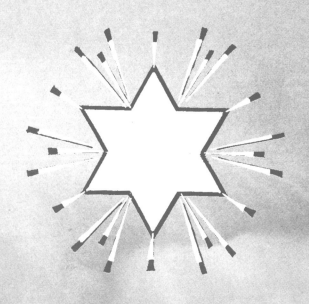

Whenever you are in need, whether your need be earthly or spiritual, always remember to visualize the golden Star shining above you and shining down into your head and your heart. Life isn't always easy, but always, always there is this beautiful, golden Star of your higher self shining above you. If you can consciously come under the Star and feel it shining down and enfolding your whole being, it will help you so much. You will feel not only the strength and protection, but also the joy, the peace and the beauty, the perfect balance of that Star.

It will help if you will
frequently visualize the Star
and the radiation of the
Star. Whenever you are
depressed, disappointed or
unhappy, if you can switch
over to the vision of the
shining Star of the spirit,
which is always there,
always shining, you will
find in that contact
all you need for your life.

According to your faith in the power of the Star to help you, whatever your need, that help will come to you. Miracles are wrought by the power of thought, and the spiritual power behind thought.

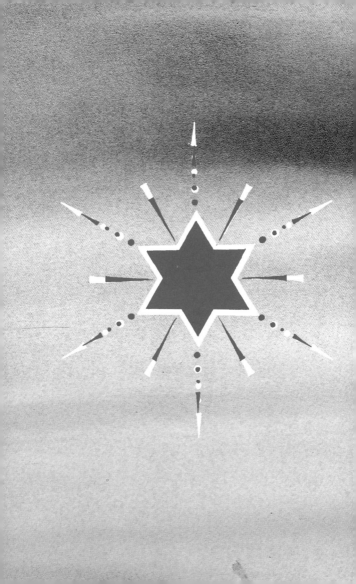

There is so much to learn about the divine magic which lies in the centre of the Star. Never doubt that the Star is permeating the whole of your physical life. Send forth the light of the Star with love and kindness; never forcing, but gently sunning and watering the seed in the heart of humanity. Persevere with your work, and you will see slowly but steadily shooting from the dark earth of materialism the little plants of green, which are little rays of light. For as nature works slowly, so does the spiritual life grow and unfold slowly and imperceptibly.

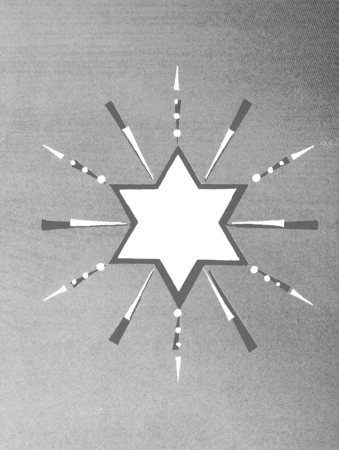

Words cannot convey to
you the power and
the love which is in the
Star; it is a truth
which each of you must
find for yourself.
The light and the power
of the Star goes forth
and is working, working,
working in the hearts
of all people. Don't be
despondent. The Star
turns all to light.

The brilliant pure Star
shines, holding you,
penetrating your soul,
strengthening you on
every level of your being.
Surrender to this
mighty love....

Darkness will not touch you if you are radiating light.

Let us see the perfect
six-pointed Star which
shines in the heart of the
Sun. We breathe in the light
from that Star until our
whole being is filled with its
light. We relax in the light of
the Star.... We are at peace,
at one with all life. See all
human kind drawn into the
heart of that Sun ... that
beautiful six-pointed Star
at the heart of the Sun.

*Wisdom, power and love;
love, wisdom and
power.... The six–pointed
Star is a symbol of
a perfect balance between
these three divine
principles.*

The Star is a symbol
of perfect being,
the inverted triangle
representing the light
which shines down to
meet the threefold
nature of every man and
woman, which is
aspiring to the highest.

By concentrating entirely
on the Star you will receive
into your mind all
the inspiration and
guidance you need for
practical decisions and
practical affairs, because
the higher triangle (your
higher, celestial self), is
putting through into the
lower triangle (your lower
self), the help you need.

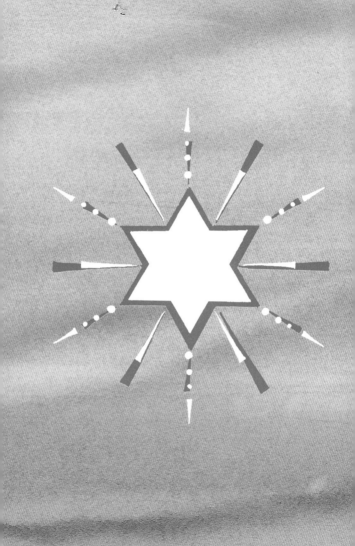

When you feel love in your
heart and then start
your work of thought-
projection, the form of the
Star which you are
projecting becomes a living
and most powerful object.
It becomes alive with the
spirit. Remember that
thought creates form, but it
is the love in your heart,
that real love in your heart,
that gives life to that form.

*As you send forth love
in the form of the Star,
it is helping to awaken
that same love, that light,
in every heart.*

Be true to the Star.
To your own higher self
be true, and then you will
find that the difficulties
of the earth life will fall
away from you and you
will be raised in
consciousness to the
level of true peace.

*Be constant and steadfast,
looking at all times into the
light of the Star. Whether you
are working alone or in a
group, keep your mind steady
and create in your soul-vision
a Star without limitation.
Whatever your personal
sorrow or difficulty, you will
gain comfort and strength
and peace of soul by
continually creating and
beholding this ever-shining
Star in the ether.*

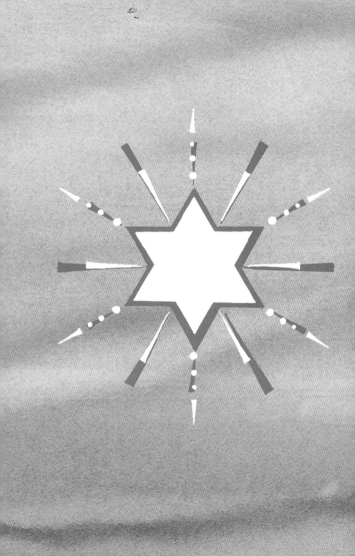

The simpler and the purer you can keep your spiritual work the better. Its strength is its simplicity, its purity and its one-pointedness. By working with the Star you are being one-pointed, but also working universally.

*Projection of the Star
means radiation of love
from your heart for all
living things, including
all the kingdoms of
nature. In projecting the
light of the Star,
remember all the aspects
of nature as well
as human life.*

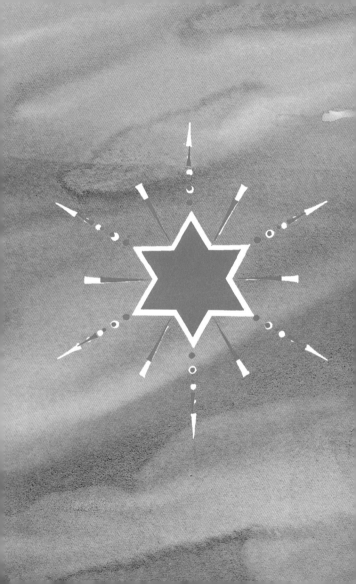

Be definite and positive in using the symbol of the Star. We ask you not so much to create a picture of the people you are trying to help (and incidentally thinking of their failures and what they don't do) but instead, to become aware of an immense, an infinite Star. Be that Star, become so full of the light of that Star that you, yourself, feel within the Star; and in that Star too behold the individual or the group or that particular work that you are hoping to help. Be very strong and true and just. Be full of love and be, yourself, in the Star.

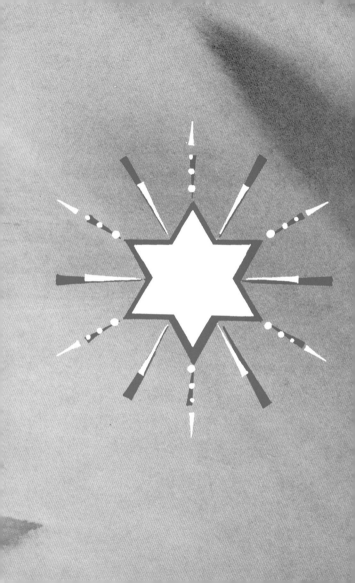

The method of working on
the inner planes is by the
power of the Star. The
very formation of the Star
on the inner planes carries
with it great power; but we
warn you that it must
never be used to dominate,
or for your own gain. It
must only be used with
love, and to help
those in need.

*Contemplate, meditate,
upon the most beautiful
jewel, the Star, on the
inner planes, blazing with
all the soft colours of
the spectrum. See the
scintillation, the pulsation
of life itself, everything the
human soul needs.
Hold your meditation
upon that Star.*

Create in your consciousness, first of all, the Star, realizing that you are in the centre of the Star. In other words, you are the Star, and from you the light goes forth into the surrounding ethers. Look up! And see the blazing light which is now pouring down upon you: blessing you, strengthening you.

*How can you send forth
the light of the Star into
the world unless the light
is shining in your heart?
This is the secret,
the key to happiness,
healthiness.*

*Endeavour constantly to
reach upwards to the
Star of wisdom, love and
power. Live in the
consciousness of its beauty.
It is the source of your life
and everyone's life; and
when you are in this Star,
when you are receiving its
power and beauty, you are
at one with all life. You and
all life are one in spirit.*

In silence there is power—the power of love, of all wisdom, all truth, lies within the silence. The manifestations of life on the outer planes are created from the silence within. Learn to seek that silence, the silence of the spirit. Do not be misled by the noise and clamour of the world. Resolutely keep your eyes upon the Star of love. It will bring you wisdom, peace.

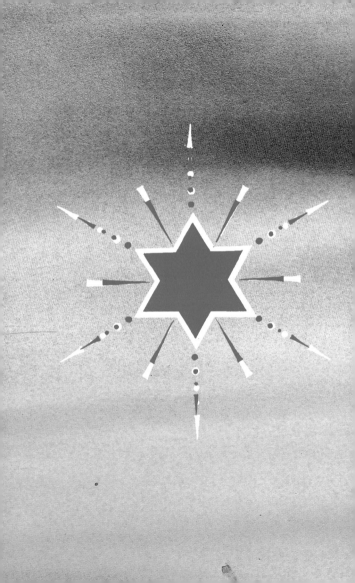

Walk quietly along the appointed way, with your eyes fixed upon the Star which leads you heavenwards. And thus your soul path will be brightened, light will flow into your heart and mind, and joy will crown your days.

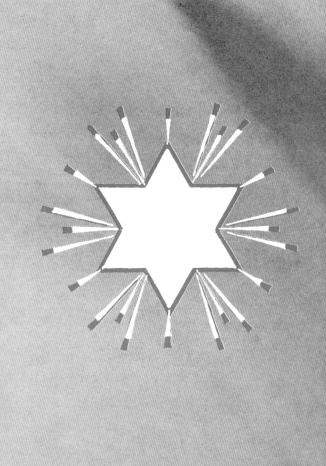

*In quiet ways
the Master works.
With quiet, steady steps
the Master walks
amongst human kind,
and you never know
when the Master
will speak to you.*

*Be calm in adversity,
be untouched by
criticism, by praise or
blame. Go steadily
forward on the path of
life, serving one another.
Follow the Star.*

*Follow where the Star
leads you. Rise above the
entanglements of the lower
mind and the material
world, and steadfastly and
positively concentrate your
heart upon the shining
Star which is above you.
Look right into it ... feel
yourself drawn into it.
Rest in the consciousness
of that shining Star.*

May the strength of the Star grow within your heart, causing you to be ever more loving and compassionate and understanding. May it cast out all fear; because that Star is your life and your support so long as you remain attuned to it.

*We know there is sorrow
in human hearts all over
the earth, but if you can
keep your heart focused
on the Star you will be
given strength and light
and wisdom—and most
of all, love, to meet every
occasion, every need.*

You will always receive
help from the Star.
Remember this, realize it,
and use the Star,
use it at all times.
Visualize the Star.

Never, in this work of the Star, work for a selfish motive to please the vanity or the greed of the lower self. It must be a positively good desire, a good object, and then the blessing will be untold.

*When your
thought-power is clear
and strong, and inspired
and infused by your
highest love in building
the Star, you are creating
the finest form through
which the forces of light
can be directed onto
the earth and into
people's hearts.*

*We ask you to hold the
vision in your heart of
all human kind being
drawn together in
brotherhood
under the Star.*

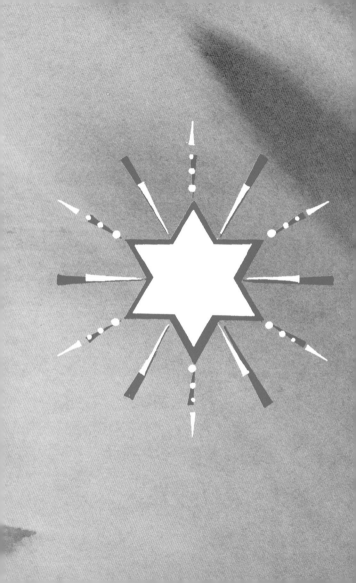

*You are stepping across
the cusp into the new age,
and this new age will see
a clearing away of that
which has outlived its
purpose. Keep your vision
upon the Star, the Star in
the heavens, and seek the
vision of the Star within
your own heart.*

The Star is the most powerful symbol which can be used for the good of humanity. It is a symbol of the perfect power and love in every human soul. Keep hope in your heart as you hold the vision of the Star, and always allow the power of love, balanced with wisdom (which shines from that Star) to guide your thoughts, your speech, your actions.

You live too much in your physical consciousness and your material world. You have to learn to balance these two lives, the life of the spirit and the life of the body. Now, if you will imagine in your heart this shining Star, this blazing jewel, we think it will help you to attain and maintain that balance between your inner and your outer life.

Think of the heavens, of the deep blue sky above you, and see the Stars shining in that canopy of the heavens.... This will help you to understand how you, as a Star—the Star in you—can give light on a dark night.

Study the symbol of the Star. Within that Star is to be found the diamond, the purest jewel of all: the jewel within the lotus of the heart; the light of pure, divine spirit.

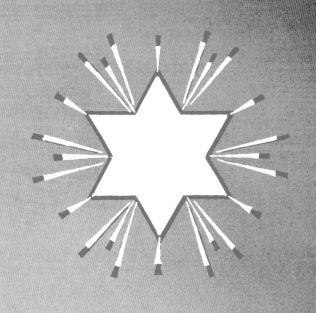

The projection of the light of the Star should not be irksome or tiring. It should be a quiet radiation from within. You are the channel for the light. You yourself form the symbol of the Star, you are the Star ... the flame.... The Star, as it radiates from your heart, calls to and stimulates the light and the love which is within the heart of those upon whom you are concentrating. The Star is like a magnet, and calls forth the light in those you would help.

You may wonder how long
it is necessary to send your
projection of the Star.
There is no time out of the
physical body. A flash
of thought, if it is alive
with love, will reach
its mark.

*The Star is built from
the pure, true love in
your hearts ... and
without the contribution
from your hearts,
there is no Star.*

Seek and reverence the light
in the heart of every soul you
meet. Remember the light
shining in the heart of the
simplest earth child;
reverence that, and help that
light in your brother–sister
to shine. So, gradually, the
light will spread throughout
the world, and the new age
of brotherhood will
truly dawn.

The mistake that all beings on earth make is to try and solve their problems by thinking of them on the physical level. Hold on to the jewel you have been given, the shining Star. It is the most powerful instrument that you have ever been given. You do not need to be anxious about any one of your loved family or friends. Hold them in the Star. You are giving them the greatest possible help, because through the Star you are helping them to help themselves.

As you, as an individual,
enter more and more into
the heart of the Star, and
live and move and have
your being in the Star,
so you will find
happiness, steadfastness,
and an unshakeable
inner strength.

Keep on keeping on with your lives, but stay simple. It is the simple love, the little candle flame, the shining Star in the heart, which is the truest guide on your path and which can be used by the shining brotherhood in the world of light to help bring healing to the nations.

When you can, even for a
short time, become still
and relaxed under the
Star of your eternal,
celestial self, you will begin
to become aware of the
presence and help of your
own guardian angel, who
is indeed an angel
of the Star.

*As you focus your
thoughts and the
innermost prayers of your
heart upon the beauty
and strength of the Star
shining in the heavens,
you will feel the presence
of angels and hear their
message as did the
shepherds on the hills of
Bethlehem, long ago.*

As we look out from the mountain height of our own perception, we see the glorious healing rays of the Star pouring light and love upon the earth and into the hearts of human kind. We see peace coming, a deeper peace than the world has ever known during the present cycle.

*It is from the quietness
of the heart that the
light of the Star radiates
across the world.*

The rising Sun–Star of the new age is shining upon the waters of the soul of humanity, bringing healing for all the world. So, let us keep our vision on the Star, and seek to work ever more closely with the shining company in the world of light to bring peace on earth and goodwill to all people.

*Be guided by your
intuition, and love;
and you will have chosen
the better path....*